BLUFF YOUR WAY IN
IN
MATHS

ROBERT AINSLEY

RAVETTE BOOKS

Published by Ravette Books Limited
3 Glenside Estate, Star Road,
Partridge Green, Horsham,
West Sussex RH13 8RA
(0403) 710392

First printed 1988
Reprinted 1991

Series Editor – Anne Tauté

Cover design – Jim Wire
Typesetting – Input Typesetting Ltd.
Printing and binding – Cox & Wyman Ltd.
Production – Oval Projects Ltd.

The Bluffer's Guides are based on
an original idea by Peter Wolfe.

CONTENTS

WHAT IS MATHEMATICS?

The word 'mathematics' comes from a Greek word meaning 'learning'. This may seem odd in view of the fact that mathematicians are usually anything but learned, and the deepest literature most of them try is *The Hitch Hiker's Guide to the Galaxy*, but it was no doubt thus named for similar reasons behind those which made the Vikings call the newly discovered island they wanted to populate quickly Greenland and not Icy Cold Miserable Barren Glacier-Ridden Land. If you want to keep interest up in the subject, you have to dress up the title a bit and make the thing sound impressive. To this end, the bluffer should always insist on the full title mathematics, and deride the American habit of referring to it as math. ("A math," you should say tersely, "ith a Roman Catholic thervithe.")

Mathematics is in a funny position, not really being accessible enough to be an Art and not being immediately useful enough to be a Science. It is generally hard to understand, goes against common sense much of the time and is far and away Public Enemy No. 1 of all the academic disciplines.

So rare is it to find someone actually good at mathematics that employers often require an O level (as it used to be) purely as a convenient way to cut down the deluge of applicants for their job roadsweeping or bus-driving or being Chancellor of the Exchequer or any of the other things which are traditionally done by people who can't add up properly. Knowing your way round mathematics will ensure instant respect; mathematicians, it is generally supposed, have the ability to think when faced with a problem. To some extent this is true – mathematicians generally have plenty of problems tackling everyday life and all most of them can do is think about it. By bluffing your way in math-

5

ematics and hence creating the impression of having an analytical, logical and clear-thinking brain you will leave others standing.

The Basics

There are a lot of books about mathematics – usually very long ones with thousands of pages of small print without pictures, full of strings of odd-looking, apparently meaningless characters – like any university maths faculty. We can, however, classify the function of mathematics quite simply. Mathematics consists essentially of:

a) proving the obvious;
b) proving the not so obvious; and
c) proving the obviously untrue.

Mathematicians are allowed to make very heavy weather of showing what everyone already knows. For example, it took mathematicians until the 1800s to prove that $1+1=2$, and not before the late 1970s were they confident of proving that any map requires no more than four colours to make it look nice, a fact known by cartographers for centuries.

There are many not-so-obvious things which can be proved true too. Like the fact that for any group of twenty-three people, there's an even chance two or more of them share a birthday. (With groups of twins this becomes almost certain. Not quite certain, as you will of course point out; they might all have been born either side of midnight).

Mathematicians are also fond of proving things which are obviously false, like all straight lines being curved, and an engaged telephone being just as likely to be free if you ring again immediately after, as if you wait twenty minutes. They also like disproving

6

things which are obviously true, for example that the shortest distance between two points on the earth's surface on an airline route always goes across Anchorage, Alaska.

Convincing people that you know your way round mathematics will unsettle them enormously and give you a psychological hand full of trump cards. To most normal people, it is a mysterious, bewildering world, a system they remember vaguely from their school days – jumbled memories of chanting times tables and problems about people filling baths without the plugs in – being apparently designed specifically to confuse them (it was). Why, they ask, do mathematicians talk about xs and ys? Why don't they call a spade a spade? Well, you can say, spades are not always spades. Sometimes spades are trumps. And most card tricks are just simple bits of mathematics anyway.

It is important to be supportive when talking about mathematics; nod sympathetically and reassure them that it's just "badly taught", that schools lack the money and resources to "make the subject come alive", and if only they could make mathematics fun, "which, of course, it can, and should be". Complete nonsense, of course; mathematics is deadly boring, as everyone knows – otherwise there wouldn't be so many books with earnest and well-meaning titles like *Matrices Can Be Fun* and *Calculus Made Easy*, which have really inspiring things on the cover like tetrahedra with x written on them. You have to imply that it is an intellectual laugh a minute if you're clever enough to appreciate it.

However, you need never attempt to justify the existence of mathematics, still less the existence of outdated school courses and text books with titles like *Essential Modern Maths*, which are always full of completely unnecessary and old-fashioned things like Venn diagrams. Mathematics is its own justification; to those who question its relevance or application you assume an imperious tone and make a comment about what a really interesting and important thing it is. Employ at random in your reply phrases like the purity of mathematics, mathematics as a tool, intrinsic patterns, a bridge between Arts and Science, training of the mind in logical thinking, etc. If some miserable quibbler should ask you a tedious question, such as 'What is the Lax-Wendroff Theorem for?' you reply testily "For? What do you mean, what's it for? It's not for anything. It is the truth". Don't fall into the trap many mathematicians set for themselves when they continue along the lines of "You might as well ask what a Beethoven symphony is for". The riposte this tends to bring is that anyone can listen to and appreciate a Beethoven symphony, whereas only a few hundred people in the world can understand the Lax-Wendroff Theorem (and very few of them could tell you what it *is* for).

Mathematics still strikes terror into the hearts of all normal sane people, and those who profess to understand any of it will instantly go up hugely in the estimation of non-bluffers. Your chances of being challenged by someone who actually knows what they're talking about are one in a million, or as the mathematician would say, almost certainly totally improbable.

Sums

There are great advantages to being a mathematician:

a) you do not have to be able to spell;
b) you do not have to be able to add up.

The illiteracy of mathematicians is taken for granted; mathematical educationists, for example, thought that 'Arithmetic' began with an 'r', along with Riting and

8

Reading (the nearest most mathematicians get to Reading is on the M4).

There still persists a myth that mathematics somehow involves numbers. Many fondly believe that university students spend their time long dividing by a hundred and seventy three, and learning their thirty-nine times table; in fact, the reverse is true. Mathematicians are renowned for their inability to add up or take away, in much the same way as geographers are always getting lost, and economists are always borrowing money off you. Never play darts with a mathematician.

You can, of course, put this entirely to your advantage; when your arithmetic is challenged, you say "I can't add up; I'm a mathematician".

Most of mathematics is, in fact, devoted to the avoidance of arithmetic; the amount of adding up, dividing and taking away decreases steadily as one progresses through a mathematical career, and the numbers one encounters disappear accordingly. Junior school children can count to a million; secondary school kids have already started replacing numbers by x and y but only use numbers up to a hundred; A level students see numerals up to ten but have substituted most numbers by letters, so much so that they have begun to run out of Roman letters and have to use Greek letters like π and α; at University, the only numbers you ever see are 0,1, and 8, except that it's written on its side, pronounced 'infinity', and means 'lots'. By this time all the letters of the alphabet have long since been used up, the Greek alphabet is just about accounted for, and those working in set theory have to start on the Hebrew alphabet and use **alephs** and **gimuls**.

The bluffer should mention in passing here that the Russians and Chinese use xs, ys, as, bs, cs and so on, in their mathematical expositions. This sort of thing strongly suggests that you are conversant with

Russian and Chinese and casually browse through the *Moscow Maths Quarterly* and the *People's Mathematical Daily* in the native languages, without actually saying so.

Non-mathematicians stand out when they try to use unknowns in propositions by being too obvious – 'Suppose I earn x amount of pounds a week,' they say. A skilled bluffer will sound infinitely more sophisticated; he or she knows the Greek letters, the Cyrillic alphabet, the odd item of Hebrew script, and slips them in whenever possible. Greek symbols in particular should be second nature to you. Use exotic letters, subscripts if possible, **theta-one** and **omega-zero**, for example: "If I earn Θ_1 pounds per week . . . "; "Let's say our company produces Ω_0 units this year. . ." etc. Good value is obtained by using brackets, to indicate one quantity is somehow dependent on the other, as in "Now suppose our productivity as a function of time is $P_\beta(t)$ . . . " This ensures instant admiration, and has the bonus that you need have no idea what you're talking about; no-one will dare argue with someone so eloquent and logically incisive. Some mathematicians insist on using the letter n to mean 'lots of', as in 'I drank n pints last night', in a feeble attempt at humour. This is a letter to avoid.

Apart from the general outlines mentioned above the question 'What is mathematics?' need not really concern you. Far better to wait for someone else to talk about it and immediately pounce on them and imply they have a vastly inferior grasp on things than you have, that they have made some howler of a misconception which is so obvious to you that you cannot begin to explain it. If they have made a genuine mistake or used a term loosely, do not let it slip. Some are obvious; when, for example, a football manager interviewed on television says the lads gave a hundred and ten per cent today, you should smile knowingly, possibly laugh quietly to yourself. When he says it is still mathematically possible for them to win the championship, you mutter "D'you mean arithmetically possible?" When he says the chances of today's result being repeated are a million to one, you say "A million to one against presumably".

Snooker gives you a good chance to show your knowledge when all the spots are covered and a colour has to be replaced 'as near to the ball which is covering its spot as possible without touching it.' The correct response here is to laugh to yourself, look down, and shake your head in resignation. If queried you say smilingly "How near is as near as possible? A millimetre? Half a millimetre? Eight and three-quarter nanometres?" and resume the shaking of the head. You will naturally know that the maximum break in snooker is 162, arising as follows: in a handicap match, giving away 155, a player takes advantage of a free ball after a foul by his opponent to pot effectively sixteen reds, sixteen blacks and the colours, and with the scores thus levelled, wins the toss to go for the respotted black first and pots it, hence making a continuous break of 162. This is a characteristically mathematical line of argument, taking a totally impossible situation to its logical conclusion.

Logic is of course the cornerstone of mathematics and you can often pick people up on sloppy use of logic, a favourite being the syllogism — 'things which are good for you taste lousy, this tastes lousy, so it must be good for you' is a good example. As you should point out, it does not follow at all, any more than it follows that 'carrots cannot drive tractors, the Empire State Building cannot drive a tractor, therefore the Empire State Building is a carrot'. In the study of formal logic it is possible to start from nothing at all but, by proceeding purely logically, show that everything is true. The most important rule of logical inference like

11

this is called **modus ponens**. Using this you can, for example, infer from the statements a) if my auntie had male chromosomes she'd be my uncle, and b) according to the tests my auntie has male chromosomes, the logical conclusion that c) therefore my auntie is my uncle. Mathematics is a very exact science and must be very rigorously applied.

As an illustration of the sort of nit-picking that is essential to a mathematician – or those wishing to appear so – it is useful to remember the story of the engineer, the physicist and the mathematician on a conference together in China. Out on a day trip, the engineer spots a black pig in a field. 'Look!' he exclaims, 'pigs in China are black!'

'No,' corrects the physicist, 'you mean, there is at least one pig in China which is black.'

'Not quite,' says the mathematician. 'You mean, there is at least one pig in China which is at least one-half black.'

Even if you can't identify a mistake as such, the moral is, challenge even vaguely mathematical statements. In order to defend your credibility as a mathematical savant, the best form of defence is attack. If you cannot make a genuine criticism, such general comments as the following will cover most situations nicely. They will give rise to grave doubt in your partner and imply some superior understanding of the situation on your part (however untrue this may be) and can be appended to almost anything, preceded, of course, by a thoughtful pause and eventual nodding of the head:

a) Well, in this case, yes . . .
b) Mm, yes, so long as the temperature/money supply/chance of precipitation/rate of inflation (anything will do, the more unrelated the better) stays constant.

c) On a basic level, yes, I suppose you could say that.

If you wish to agree wholeheartedly with a proposition, again imply some higher level of intuition, as in:

d) Yes. . . . in fact, that holds for all similar cases, doesn't it?

Figures are excellent ground for query. You can catch anyone out on anything if they try to quote figures. Good ones to use are:

a) These figures are interesting I suppose – but they don't really tell you anything do they?
b) They seem a bit rough – too rough, if you ask me.
c) They seem fairly accurate – suspiciously accurate, if you ask me.

Should you yourself be challenged, look as if you can't possibly imagine how anyone could fail to understand your viewpoint and claim that "It's obvious".

MEN OF MATHEMATICS

Mathematics being generally either right or wrong, its great men are above criticism, because all the work they produced was right (well, almost all of it, anyway). Hence you cannot really try to classify them into good and bad, or ones you like and ones you don't, as you would with composers, though you can often demonstrate your knowledge of their private lives to good effect. Knowing that Newton died a virgin will count for much more at most parties than being able to prove the binomial theorem.

As a bright practitioner you will always have the big names ready to drop into any conversation and be conversant with the work of the great men, in name at least. No-one will ever have the confidence to challenge you to prove Leibniz's Theorem, or to integrate sine x; the names are always enough.

The Babylonians
Invented time, which the Egyptians never got round to doing. Because they counted up to fifty-nine as normal but then, for some inconceivable reason, counted in units of sixty from there on, the world has had sixty seconds in a minute and sixty minutes in an hour ever since. For similar reasons linked to astronomy there are three-hundred and sixty degrees in a circle and three hundred and sixty days in a year, plus five and a bit. The Babylonians knew about Pythagoras' Theorem in a rough and ready sort of way but had never realised its potential to terrorise school children and neglected to follow it up.

Thales (fl. 585 B.C.)
The first mathematician. He invented proofs and a bit of geometry, and on discovering his fourth proposition (that a triangle drawn in a semi-circle is always a

right angled triangle) was so pleased that he went out and made a sacrifice to the Gods: a bull. Geometry has appeared that way to many people ever since.

Pythagoras (fl. 530 B.C.)

The second mathematician. Populariser of the right angled triangle and the first person to breed a hypotenuse in captivity, Pythagoras was famous for scratching out diagrams in the sand. It was here that he discovered the world's first theorem – that the square of the hypotenuse is equal to the sum of the squares of the other two sides. He met his end when he told a Roman soldier to stop walking over his hypotenuses and the soldier, who decided he couldn't stand a smart-arse, killed him. This was rather a shame, because Pythagoras led his own commune who sat around in the sun all day drinking and talking about infinity, and seems to have been quite a hippy.

The Romans were not much good at mathematics. They used Roman numerals to perform calculations, and had a patently ridiculous way of handling fractions. Their system of writing mathematics was even more cumbersome than the Greeks, who just wrote everything out longhand. They were much more concerned with building central heating systems and viaducts and earning money than sitting around in the sun all day talking about infinity. They set the pattern for engineers to come.

There are, of course, several hundred different ways of proving Pythagoras' Theorem, so if you have to bluff your way through a proof of it, almost anything will do. Scratch a few plausible-looking triangles and squares in the sand or on the dashboard or on the restaurant tablecloth, keep mentioning the words 'hypotenuse', 'area' and 'square', and make sure that, at the most obscure and incomprehensible step in the proof, you use the mathematician's trick of saying "Now here's the clever bit".

Euclid (fl. 350 B.C.)

Produced a definitive work on all geometry in a series of books called *Elements*. In this, Euclid designed the first straight lines, points and plane, the Euclidean plane. Sadly on its maiden flight, it flew too close to the sun and the wings melted.

In the final book of this huge work he introduced the Platonic solids. Most solid shapes before Plato (eggs, balls, lumps of putty, etc.) had been used by the Greeks for a variety of unsavoury activities, but he put a stop to this by inventing this new set of objects to be used platonically. These are geometric shapes made out of polystyrene, and occur naturally in Open University broadcasts. They are all perfectly regular and have a number of faces, like a good politician (and politics was also, of course, invented in Greece). There are only five known to man – the four-sided **tetrahedron** (common), the six-sided **hexahedron** or cube (common), the eight-sided **octahedron** (rare), a thing with twelve sides (**dodecahedron** – very rare), and a twenty-sided thing (the **icosahedron**, which is not found outside trivia quizzes). The wise bluffer will, of course, know these names off by heart. Faced with the difficulty of finding a name for an object with more than twenty sides, Plato desisted from designing any more.

Archimedes (c287–212 B.C.)

The greatest of the Greek mathematicians, Archimedes sprang to fame when he ran naked through the streets of Greece shouting 'Eureka', which means 'I've found it.' He had just worked out **Archimedes' Principle**, which states that when a body is immersed naked in water, it experiences an upthrust. Or so he claimed in court.

Archimedes was both an engineer and a mathematician, and in addition to designing pumps and screws did much work in mathematics and would have discovered calculus two thousand years before Newton did, if only algebra had been invented. He didn't think much of engineering however, and much preferred the theoretical purity of mathematics, setting the pattern for mathematicians to come. He was concerned with higher things, meaningful things, like calculating the number of grains of sand in the universe; the answer he got was one followed by sixty-three noughts.

The compleat bluffer always knows about the obscure as well as the famous – in fact, the more obscure the better, in order to convince even experts that you know your subject in depth. So, the next mathematician to come along is of course our old friend:

Al-Khwarizmi (fl. 830)
With a name like this under your belt you can bluff your way past even a bona fide mathematician. The Romans had never got round to inventing zero, and hence lacked no-score draws; it took many hundreds of years for this situation to be rectified. This Arab was the first to use zero (one of the commonest Arabic words in English after coffee and hashish), from the name of the empty row on the abacus, in a major mathematical work. This was a great step forward; it meant the development of place values – thousands, hundreds, tens, units. (In fact, the concept of zero and place values had been developed by the Hindu mathematicians in the court of King Ashoka a couple of hundred years earlier.)

He also began to use the system of writing numerals called **Arabic numerals** – so called because it was the

Arabs who first had the brilliant idea of nicking them from the Hindus. This new system scored heavily over the old Roman numerals in that never again would clever dicks insist on writing the year out as MCDMLLXXXXIVIIVI or ask you which letter represented ten million. Incidentally, the Romans used to write 'four hundred and forty-four', for example, as CCCCXXXXIIII and not CDXLIV, which was a mediaeval development to save paper.

Another significiant advance in mathematics achieved by the Arabs (mainly in fact, by Al-Khwarizmi again) was **Kitab al-mukhtasar fi'l-hisab al-jabr wa'l-muqabalah**. When the person you are talking to asks in bewilderment what this is, feign astonishment that they've never heard of it and say "Why, algebra, of course."

Negative numbers were probably first devised soon after by an unnamed group of Hindu economists who immediately put their discovery to good use by inventing overdrafts. It was a long time before negative numbers were regarded as legitimate in the west, and only a run of desperately cold Greenland-like winters in the middle ages convinced people that subzeros were for real.

The Chinese, meanwhile, despite supposedly being the most advanced civilisation because they had invented fireworks, paper and the Civil Service, seem to have achieved little in mathematics. The nearest they had to a zero was the character meaning 'nothing' which had thirteen strokes and took so long to write that it was easier just to lie and write the much quicker single stroke for 'one'. They thus lacked the neat Arabic system and lagged behind in commerce, failed to export paper to the West causing serious shortages, had no coffee trade at all, and lost the Opium War.

Galileo Galilei (1564–1642)

This Italian shocked and amazed the world when he dropped two balls from the top of the Leaning Tower of Pisa. He did this to prove objects of different weights falling to the ground hit the earth at the same time (unsuccessful previous demonstrations involved dropping two spheres, one a pound of lead, and one a pound of iron. It was not until many years later that the fault was discovered). If your bluffee challenges you on *why* a ten-ton weight should drop to earth at the same speed as a feather when it clearly does not, you should mumble something about air resistance and offer to demonstrate your point by dropping a heavy object (say one of their cut-glass vases) and a light object (say a teaspoon) together from the top of the stairs. They will suddenly accept the theory without the need for demonstration.

Galileo was also at the centre of a ghastly misunderstanding when he was overheard talking to his wife about the earth moving. He was accused of heresy by the Catholic Churchmen of the time and made to sign a confession stating that the earth did not move.

René Descartes (1596–1650)

Inventor of Cartesian coordinates and not wells, this Frenchman was one of the first great bluffers. 'Are you sure about this?' his tutors would ask of his ideas on analytic geometry. 'Well, I *think* it's true, therefore it is,' he would reply. He went on to make a lot of money out of this idea, and changed to the more lucrative study of philosophy. His work reduced all geometry just to long strings of numbers, a remarkably prophetic concept in view of the fact that computers were over three centuries away. So influential was Descartes that his model of the solar system, completely inaccurate so as to please the Catholic Church, was accepted and held back any progress in astronomy for decades.

Pierre Fermat (1601–1675)
Another first-class French bluffsmith. Fermat only took to mathematics as a hobby; by profession he was a lawyer, so he was well versed in concepts of logical argument, truth, and how to twist it around. He is famous for **Fermat's Last Theorem**, a by-word for bluffers everywhere. In a letter to a friend concerning the problem of proving that no integer solutions for n above 2 exist of the equation

$$a^n + b^n = c^n$$

he wrote in the margin 'I have discovered a marvellous proof of this, but the margin is not big enough to contain it.'

Even today no-one has managed to prove it for all values of n, though some persistent mathematicians, with nothing better to do, have proved it for every number less than a hundred except for 37, 59 and 67. No-one really knows if Fermat did indeed have an incredibly sneaky proof which we haven't hit upon yet, or if he was just bluffing.

Kowa Seki (1642–1708)
Another mathematician so obscure that few mathematicians have even heard the name; you can look surprised at their ignorance of this Japanese who almost single handedly and virtually from scratch discovered everything in algebra and calculus known in the West, much of it in advance of his occidental counterparts. He did this despite there being virtually no tradition in the subject in the East at that time, and he had to devise his own notation to do so.

Given that any Japanese trying to leave the country, or any foreigner entering Japan, was executed during this period, Kowa's ability to work unaided was just as well. In addition he was a great teacher and populariser of mathematics, and for a laugh worked out the value of π correct to eighteen decimal places, the most accurate value at that time available anywhere in the world, except on a German gravestone.

Isaac Newton (1642–1727)

Newton's mother tried to withdraw him from school in Woolsthorpe, Lincolnshire when he was fourteen to be a farmer but he went on to Trinity College, Cambridge instead. During the plague he returned home and it was here that he saw an apple fall from a tree and from it, by an incredible stroke of genius, worked out the laws governing the motion of everything in the universe. You should of course know that the apple story is true, and came to us via no less than Voltaire, who got it from Newton's step-niece, a Mrs Conduitt.

In the course of all this he invented calculus but because he called it fluxions it never took off, and nothing was published. Seven years later the German mathematician **Leibniz** rediscovered calculus, but had the wisdom to call it **calculus** (after the Greek word for 'pebble', which Archimedes would have called calculus, had algebra been invented to enable him to discover it) and published his findings. He put his claim for the copyright to a committee of famous mathematicians, not knowing that one of them was, surprise, surprise, Newton. Hence Newton's prior claim was confirmed, though Leibniz's notation was adopted.

The sign for integration $\int$ comes from the old form of 's' used in this period which resembled an 'f', an **integral** being, of course, a fum of a feries of fmall numbers.

Newton published his great work, the *Principia Mathematica*, in 1687, in which he set out the laws controlling everything. You can talk knowledgeably of Newton's clockwork universe which is, as Einstein demonstrated, a load of rubbish.

The **Bernouilli Bros. of Basle** (Jacques (1654–1705) and Jean (1667–1748))

This wacky pair invented the **Calculus of Variations**, totally independently but at the same time, which they used to prove everything, for example viaducts and ski-slopes. Two good words to drop in to the conversation while talking about these two are **brachistochrone** (a curve whose shape means you slide down in the shortest time) and **tortochrone** (a curve such that, if a pendulum moved in this shape, it would keep perfect time). You certainly won't get any other chance to use them.

They hated each other's guts.

Abraham de Moivre (1667–1754)

A friend of Newton's who developed the theory of mortality, annuities and life assurance. He invented **n!**. N! is used a lot in probability and gaming theory and de Moivre worked as a consultant for gambling syndicates and insurance companies on the basis of n! to finance his drinking. He died of drink in poverty; actuaries take note.

Laplace/Legendre/Lagrange (c1740–c1820)

Three easily confused Frenchmen – anyone spending their life in mathematics is usually quite confused anyway. All you have to remember are the phrases Laplace Transforms, Legendre Polynomials and Lagrange Multipliers. If you can consistently remember which name goes with which thing you will be doing better than most.

Karl Gauss (1777–1855)

At the age of three Gauss was correcting his father's arithmetic, and in his first lesson at school he completed the task set by a mean teacher to add up all the numbers from 1 to 100 in one minute. He did lots of work in all areas of mathematics and co-invented the telegraph, and was to many people the brainiest mathematician, if not the brainiest human being, ever.

William Hamilton (1805–1865)

The mathematician from Dublin who invented **quaternions**. Hamilton was walking along a canal in the Irish countryside one day when he suddenly had a brainwave:

$$i^2 = j^2 = k^2 = ijk = -1$$

So pleased was he with this idea that he scratched it on the nearest bridge, where it remains to this day. This is a particularly beautiful piece of mathematics; no-one has ever really found a good use for it, but it looks very nice on paper, if a little incongruous on stone bridges.

You will of course know that Hamilton invented Lagrangian Mechanics, and Lagrange invented Hamiltonian mechanics.

Hamilton spoke more than ten languages and was an alcoholic.

Evariste Galois (1811–1832)

One of the most interesting mathematicians ever. He was jailed for anti-royalist activities in the revolution in 1831, and was killed in a duel at the age of twenty, having written up everything he knew the night before lest it be lost to mankind. He didn't finish writing until dawn and was so tired he couldn't shoot straight. Galois did a lot of work in algebra and that sort of thing, and had the brilliant idea of just making up fictitious numbers to supply answers to problems which didn't otherwise have a solution, a splendid bluffing device. Simply knowing that he invented **Galois Theory** ("which is very hard to understand") will be enough for all practical purposes.

Gottlob Frege (1846–1925)

Surely the unluckiest mathematician in the world, and not just because his father couldn't spell. He had just received the galley proofs of *Grundgesetze der Arithmetik*, his life's work, in 1903 when he got a letter from Bertrand Russell who noted that due to a mistake in the initial structures Frege had set up to try and describe all of mathematics completely and logically, there was a paradox (now called **Russell's Paradox**) and the entire book, and Frege's life work, was therefore completely wrong. Undeterred Frege went gamely ahead and published the book with a note in the back to the effect that, while the entire work was wrong, he hoped people would find it interesting anyway.

William Gossett (1876–1937)

You should know that the foundation for much of statistics – the theory of errors, sampling and so on – was laid by this man, who worked for Guinness in Dublin, and published his work under the pen-name 'student', because in those days, being a student actually had more street credibility than working in a brewery.

Bertrand Russell (1872–1970)

English mathematician and philosopher who is remembered by serious mathematicians for having written *Principia Mathematica* in 1910 along with Alfred North Whitehead, in which they managed to make mathematics logical (which it hadn't been up till then, one presumes). Among his lesser known works is *In Praise of Idleness*. In 1950 he won the Nobel Prize for literature – an extraordinary feat for a mathematician.

Albert Einstein (1879–1955)

Einstein did not talk at all till the age of three, did not speak at all well until he was nine, got expelled from his school in 1894 for being 'disruptive', hated exams, only got into the Swiss Institute of Technology at the second attempt, was a failure there, and eventually became a Technical Clerk (third class) in the Swiss Patent Office, where he started his famous work on relativity. If you know this it will impress much more than being able to explain the Lorentz transformation, derive $E=mc^2$ or work out the speed of light. It also provides plenty of encouragement to parents, and to anyone who hates exams.

Einstein was persuaded into helping along atom bomb research, much to his later regret. He was awarded the Nobel prize in 1921 for his work on quantum theory, and offered the premiership of Israel in 1952, but refused.

The last thirty years of his life were spent being a pacifist and trying to work out **unified field theory** – one equation which describes everything in the universe – but he never quite managed it.

The story goes that Einstein's brain is still preserved in a jar somewhere in a University cupboard in California. It has never come on the market for sale so its value cannot be determined, but it probably would not fetch as much as the average mathematics undergraduate's brain which, of course, has hardly been used.

Kurt Goedel (1906–1978)

An Austrian who depressed everyone in the trade by showing in 1930 that there's no way of actually proving mathematics isn't just a load of lies.

MATHEMATICS IN EDUCATION

There is, of course, a dearth of good mathematics teachers – no wonder; anyone smart enough to understand compound interest and applied statistics will be off applying his or her knowledge in the City and making money out of it. Why subject themselves to a lifetime surrounded by a pandemonium of fresh-faced young people in uniform shouting to each other across the classroom for nine grand a year, they say, when they can do exactly the same in the trading room of any stockbrokers for ninety?

In the light of this, O level maths is now a requirement for all teachers, so that games masters and geography mistresses can be pressed into service in the maths department.

All of which means that in the lower years of education a child is increasingly likely to be taught mathematics by a non-mathematician. This is a splendid development as it means it is that much more possible to bluff one's way past most teachers right up to University – and thence to a firm of stockbrokers.

Primary School

Mathematics is huge fun at primary school. Children cut out shapes, add up with little blocks of wood, run round the classroom pretending to be decimal points, etc. Bluffing here is straightforward. Few teachers can spot the five- or seven-sided hexagon in the middle of a pattern. And the tendency to write numbers the wrong way round can make 2 and 5, 4 and 9, 1 and 7, 3 and 8, interchangeable. Very useful for doubling the possibilities of the answer you write down.

Secondary School

Much of mathematics teaching is still done by the ancient chalk-and-blackboard method. There are two types of blackboard, to go with the two types of mathematics teacher – the old type which is fixed and rigid and never moves an inch and the new type which goes round and round in circles. Neither fulfils the simple role of providing legible information and the wise child will sit right at the back of the class where he or she can blame all their mistakes on not being able to see the question properly.

For the first time books become very important. It is an interesting feature of mathematics books that the titles imply that the subject gets easier as one goes along. While the fourteen-year-olds are using *Advanced Algebra*, the sixteen-year-olds have *Simple Higher Algebra* and the eighteen-year-olds are on *Algebra: Some Elementary Perspectives on Group Theory*.

The most important book to have, of course, is the answer book. Any local bookshop will supply the answer book version of the course book, and once again, the 'black and white' nature of mathematics comes to the bluffer's aid. If the answers to the homework are all correct, it is impossible to prove that they weren't reached legitimately.

There will be times, of course, when keen teachers set problems which are not in any book. The technique here is to have a table of random answers ready, such as:

$$1)\ \sqrt{3}/2;\ 2)\ 60\ °;\ 3)\ \pm 1;\ 4)\ 2x$$

So long as the overall appearance of the answers is plausible enough, few teachers will be concentrating enough as they watch Sportsnight to notice that none of the answers corresponds with a question. Even if a wrong answer is spotted it will always look reasonable enough to 'show you're thinking.'

If in doubt, draw a picture. It is well-known that individuals' perception of the world can be very different, so it is difficult to say someone's drawing of the path taken by a man X crossing a river R from points A to B is wrong – pass it off as an interpretation. You can prove anything with a picture, and probably will. Certainly a small diagram, preferably upside-down, labelled with large criss-crossing arrows on the page after the relevant problem and crammed into one corner of the margin, will impress examiners no end. So long as you are seen to be visualising the situation in your mind's eye, however idiosyncratically, you will get the benefit of any doubt – and examiners are always in doubt.

A Level

There is a bewildering number of A levels available – Pure Maths, Applied Maths, Pure & Applied Maths, Pure Maths with Statistics, etc., etc. For the first time the subject splits into two sections:

1. Pure Mathematics
The aim of pure mathematics is to get beautiful results on paper by ignoring real life; the shorter and more compact the result, the better. Hence, pure mathematicians tend to look down on Applied Mathematics, with its three-foot-long equations trying to describe the movement of water down a bath plug, as a grovelling and unwieldy subject getting dangerously close to engineering. They drink wine, play chess, listen to Bach, and put pictures by Maurits Escher on their study walls.

2. Applied Mathematics
This branch aims to produce models describing how things work and by trying to describe systems more and more accurately gets longer and longer equations so that they frequently spill over several pages. Applied mathematicians look down on pure mathematicians as ivory tower dreamers. They drink beer, play darts, listen to Dire Straits, and put girlie calendars or snoopy posters on their study walls.

A level maths is, of course, quite different in approach. For a start, you are expected to prove things at this level and so the sure-fire method of drawing pictures no longer holds water, even for men crossing rivers. Random answers can still be used, but should be tailored to the needs of A level, hence your typical answers might now be:

$$1)\ e;\quad 2)\ \pi;\quad 3)\ \infty;\quad 4)\ x^n;$$

... where numbers have largely been replaced by letters.

Copying also becomes more difficult as not only the answer but also the working out becomes important. So, in order to get maximum credit for your working out, you should include as many techniques as possible in your method. Refer to any or all of the following and you are bound to be on the right track somewhere.

Proof by Induction
A very important and powerful mathematical tool, because it works by assuming something is true and then goes on to prove that therefore it is true. Not surprisingly, you can prove almost anything by induction. So long as the proof includes the following phrases:

 a) Assume true for n; then also true for n+1,

because (followed by some plausible but messy working out in which n, n+1 appear prominently)
b) But is true for n=0 (a little more messy working out with lots of zeros sprayed at random through the proof)
c) So is true for all n Q.E.D.

Take logs

Broadly speaking, any equation which looks difficult will look much easier when logs are taken on both sides. Taking logs on one side only is tempting for many equations but may be noticed.

$\sin^2 + \cos^2 = 1$

You can say this any time during a proof and it will always be relevant. In fact, this is just Pythagoras' Theorem, written in a more impressive way. This being the first and most favourite of all theorems, you get bonus points just for sentimental value.

Reductio ad Absurdum

By assuming something is false and showing this leads to a contradiction, you can assume it must have actually been true in the first place. This method of proof is called reductio ad absurdum. In practice it means that whenever a contradiction (for 'contradiction' read 'cock-up') arises anywhere, you need only write "reductio ad absurdum, hence the proof holds".

At the end of a proof you write Q.E.D., which stands not for quod erat demonstrandum as the books would have you believe, but for Quite Easily Done. After a diagram you have drawn to prove something by actually constructing it, you write Q.E.F., which stands similarly not for quod erat faciendum, but Quite Easily Fiddled.

University Entrance Exams

The easiest exams to bluff your way through, because they rest on the excellent principle that the best way of solving a problem is the most economical, which is usually found out by mathematicians who can't be bothered to churn through the standard, long-winded methods, often summed up as 'a lazy mathematician is a good mathematician'. Certainly Oxford and Cambridge tutors are, on that score, very, very good mathematicians indeed.

You can put this to your advantage by being as lazy as possible in the exam papers. Answers should be the minimum length and include phrases like:

- by symmetry, we can show that . . .
- it is obvious that . . .
- intuitively, we can see that . . .
- by continuity, we know that . . .
- summing to infinity, we get . . .
- taking logs, differentiating, squaring both sides, rearranging, solving, integrating, and taking roots, then, we have . . .

and so on, with the answer appearing like magic in the shortest possible time. Here your table of random answers will look like:

- Yes, but this is more than the number of grains of sand in the universe
- Never
- The answer is imaginary
- The answer is irrational
- The answer is irrational and imaginary
- Solutions to this are all trivial
- Solutions to this are all nontrivial
- Solutions to this only exist in nine

dimensions/complex numbers/your own warped imagination, etc.

Note that not only all numbers, but all symbols have disappeared completely.

University

You will be expected to be something of a professional mathematician at university, and you should choose your image accordingly. There are three sharply defined groups of university mathematician which we will number 0, 1 and ∞ (the numbers 2 and 3 do not, of course, exist in university mathematics).

Type 0

You are either very short or very tall with greasy hair. The only evidence for your existence is a huge list of books out of the library in your name and a stream of Bach playing in your room on a Sunday morning. You never ever indulge in any sports more strenuous than solving one of Rubik's puzzles, though you may well score for the university second cricket team and know all the team members' averages to four decimal places. You probably go on to do a PhD though you are not quite sure why. You have never had any sort of girl-friend or boyfriend. You hate drunken socialising in the company of people with whom you have nothing in common, and yet on graduating either become a don or an accountant.

Type 1

The vast majority of mathematicians are type one. You wear steel-framed glasses, watch *Dr. Who* and

Star Trek and occasionally buy a new pair of jeans. You like mainstream rock and heavy metal and tend to drink too much at parties. Your boy/girlfriend is also a mathematician and you don't like admitting that you can't solve any of Rubik's puzzles. You put "I have a sense of humour" on your cv. If male, your name is Nick, Dave or Chris. You cannot be bothered to read any further than B in the careers manuals, so that after graduating you become an accountant, an actuary or a banker.

Type ∞

A tiny fraction of mathematicians are the infinitely unpredictable class. You chose mathematics because you don't have to do essays, because you can't write. You are quick to point out that mathematics therefore takes the least time to do per week out of all subjects, because you can "either do it or you can't".

Genuine type infinity mathematicians are never ever seen around college but play soccer and cricket for the university first team, have lost count of their girlfriends and boyfriends none of whom are anything to do with mathematics, are quite proud to tell you they neither know nor care who Rubik is, and on graduating become absolutely anything except an accountant, an actuary or a banker.

Having chosen your character you can then proceed to bluff your way through three years of university life as follows.

Constructing Solutions

Occasionally the worst may come to the worst and you cannot find the solution anywhere. Here you have to rely on several well-tried and tested techniques for making incoherent answers look plausible:

Page-turning Method

An old favourite which can still keep working for you right up to finals. Suppose you know what you have to prove, and also know how to start, but cannot link the two up however you try. All you do is to work back as far as you can from the answer, and down as far as you can from the question, engineering your pages such that the break occurs across the turn of a page. You can enhance the effect by making sure this break takes you from page two, say, to halfway down page nine, thus spreading the gap across ten minutes of searching time and rendering it almost imperceptible.

Change of Variables Method

Interesting historically because it harks back to primary school when bad handwriting could turn 2s into 5s and so on. Here you have a staggering range of letters to choose for use in your proofs – a to z, α to ω, even Cyrillic Я and Ж and И, or Hebrew characters if you prefer. Hence there is infinite scope for creative use of these symbols, changing one into another if the need arises in the middle of a proof. The skilful bluffer can perform wonders of transformation here, changing an x to a χ, and α to δ via 0, and b to β by way of 8 and S. In this way you can not only change one thing into another but, by judicious cancelling-out, get rid of unwanted letters completely, or introduce totally new ones if you prefer. This is a powerful mathematical tool with many applications in wide-ranging areas of the subject.

MacDonald's Lemma

Lemmas are 'mini-theorems', proved before a really big theorem as a sort of tool to use later. They should not be confused with the suicidal furry mammals called lemmings, which are about as useful in mathematics as a lemma is in real life. All you need know about lemmas is that **Burnside's Lemma** was absolutely nothing at all to do with Burnside. If you are in a confident mood you can even assert it is not actually a lemma either, just as a Peking Duck does not really come from Bombay and is not a fish.

There has never been a mathematician of any renown by the name of MacDonald so this is a standard choice of name to use for a lemma or theorem which you need but doesn't exist. For example, if, during the course of your solution, your proof requires that "All deformed hypernodules have an infinitely warped subnodule" (which may or may not be true, you neither know nor care), you merely state this at the appropriate point in your exposition.

"Now, by MacDonald's Lemma, we know that all deformed hypernodules have a subnodule which is infinitely warped. Hence. . . ." and away you go.

MacDonald's Lemma, or Theorem, is very useful but should not be overused – don't use it twice on the same page to say different things, for example.

You could try as a variation the corollary of MacDonald's Theorem. A corollary is a spasmodic fit under whose influence a mathematician suddenly decides to apply a theorem backwards.

Proof by Assumption
Another powerful technique. Assume the result you want is true, and go on to prove that, if this is the case, then the proposition you are trying to prove holds, which proves the original assumption, i.e. that the result you want is true. Thus the problem is solved.

Do not underestimate this one; many of the great mathematicians in history have used it more often than is generally let on. It requires a little thought and careful wording but the line of reasoning can usually be made tortuous enough to get past even the most attentive tutor as he or she sits in the pub/Bach concert/kitchen at a party marking your work.

Giving Wrong Answers

Rather than sit and look confused and say I don't know, the smart bluffer will appear to get a flash of inspiration when asked a question he or she doesn't understand in the slightest and give a random answer confidently. The great thing is that mathematics can be so complex at this level that very often the difference in working which would eventually result in the answer being the right one or a random letter of the Cyrillic alphabet can be minimal. A good tutor will try desperately to reconstruct from your answer what thought-processes you must have followed, and this can take anything up to half an hour.

Asking the Not Quite Totally Irrelevant Question

Most tutors love talking and will be happy to answer any questions you may have – the art is to ask questions not actually irrelevant to the subject of study, but ones which need no knowledge to be able to discuss. As examples try:

1. I see the man behind this theorem came from Norway (China, Burkina Faso, etc.) . . . is there a tradition of mathematics there?
2. Could this theorem have been discovered without Euclidean geometry?
3. Is it possible to prove this using a computer? etc.

Topics for Discussion

Mathematicians are a pretty boring lot on the whole and find it difficult to talk about anything non-mathematical. Put this to your advantage. If anyone asks you what mathematics at university 'is like', your first line of defence is to claim that it's all awfully dry and dusty and uninteresting to the layman and difficult to understand even for the expert, so you won't bore them by talking about it. If pressed, however, you can claim to have studied the following:

Chaos
Chaos proves the existence of free will and sounds awfully interesting, even if it may not be very important. It is a new area in mathematics and hence must always be described as exciting.

Fourier Series
Almost anything is, or can be, a Fourier Series. They are not very interesting, but are very important.

Differential Equations
Differential equations crop up everywhere and are, of course, very, very important, and quite interesting. They are usually pretty tricky to solve, but not as tricky as partial differential equations. There is only one interesting application of differential equations, which is working out the fluctuations in numbers of sharks breeding at a certain rate who eat fish at such and such a rate who breed at so and so speed. Exotic variations exist with populations of cockroaches, spiders, lemmings etc.

Vector Space
There is plenty of vector space in mathematics and it comes in all shapes and sizes from points to sheets up

to three, four or indeed any number of dimensions. However few university blackboards can cope with four dimensional space so this tends to be neglected. Vector space is very important and very interesting, but not as much as Hilbert space, which has been sold before now to gullible tourists in jars just as unscrupulous locals used to sell Loch Ness Monster Eggs and haggis feathers. Hilbert space is, of course, simply a vector space in which every Cauchy sequence converges. State this with a straight face and it's guaranteed to put down almost anyone who dares challenge you.

Set Theory
Set theory is not only very interesting, but is also incredibly important, because it is the foundation for everything in mathematics. You can prove, for example, the existence of numbers, which is useful, and even show that one and one makes two. It usually takes at least until the third year of an undergraduate course to do this. You will of course know Russell's Paradox ("Is the set of all sets which are not members of themselves, a member of itself?" – learn this by heart and you can destroy a conversation at fifty paces) which for a time looked dangerously as though it would prove that all mathematics was false. Fortunately the rules of set theory were redesigned to circumvent this and world can sleep safe in the knowledge that numbers probably do exist after all.

Probability
Problems in university probability are always set in infinite car parks in which there is a drunk taking a random walk. It is very interesting and extremely important to those trying to remember where in the pub car park they left their car.

Fluid Mechanics

Good terms here (all clearly very important and extremely interesting) are:

bifurcation – The phenomenon of smoke rising up straight and then for no apparent reason wiggling out into little ripples. "The mathematics is very complex," you say, implying you actually understand it when, in fact, no-one does.

Coriolis Force – The force that makes bathwater go clockwise down the plug hole in the northern hemisphere, or is it the south, nobody can remember, as a consequence of the earth spinning, except that it isn't, because the shape of the bath makes all the difference.

matched wave asymptotics – "For use in harnessing wave power in the UK", you can say, "but its big use in the US is in military combat." While not entirely true it sounds plausible nevertheless.

Solid Mechanics

Be disparaging about solid mechanics. It is neither interesting nor important. Say it's just a heap of vibrating plates and dismiss it contemptuously as being mere engineering ("and look what happened to the Tacoma Bridge," you can declare, referring to the bridge which shook itself to bits in a gale in the sixties). Remember a mathematician holds an engineer in roughly the same esteem as a lemming; both are woolly and jump to unfortunate conclusions.

MATHEMATICS IN REAL LIFE

Opportunities abound for the bluffer to display his or her knowledge of the mathematics behind the real world. Mathematicians themselves tend to suffer from a firm belief that their subject is obscure and inaccessible and has no relevance to real life. True though this undoubtedly is on the whole, there are still many occasions when you can refer to some mathematical idea, or reel off a couple of meaty technical terms and bring the subject alive (but note with caution that the last person to bring a subject alive was Dr Frankenstein).

You can claim that anything is just simple mathematics really: card tricks, snooker, running a business, playing chess, deciding which order to do one's tasks for the day, etc. This all falls down, of course, because mathematicians are invariably pretty hopeless at all of these (except chess – which is nothing to do with everyday life) but it is a good line to take, and one which is impossible to disprove. Even behind flower-arranging or playing hunt the thimble or training gerbils to ride unicycles there must be some beautiful mathematical principles, such as the ones no-one's bothered to discover because they've got along quite happily without them until now.

People generally have a low opinion of mathematics and especially of mathematicians, regarding them as a special breed with flares and steel-rimmed glasses and an appallingly bad sense of humour. This is rather unfair; many mathematicians wear contact lenses, for example. But the untouchable nature of the subject is partly due to its unapproachability, and this is exacerbated by the fact that it appears so humourless. Very rare indeed is the mathematician who could be called a wit, and unfortunately the existence of any number of half-wits cannot make up for this.

This is just one example of the non-arithmetic nature of everyday life – two halves not making a whole. If this was always so it would be possible to have two and a half brothers, for example, by having one brother and three half-brothers. Often, of course, the whole is more than the sum of the parts (despite conclusive proofs to the contrary by set theoreticians in the nineteenth century) as in a restaurant when everyone's paid their share and yet it doesn't come to the figure indicated on the bill. And everyone knows that two wrongs don't make a right – even though they should, the composition of two negatives being positive, of course.

For the bluffer it is essential to know these situations where mathematics fails, and to know the rule which is being disobeyed. In this way you will give the impression of not only being practical and in touch with the world, but also knowing the deep and meaningful principles behind it, which ought to be being followed.

Proportionality

One of the most common mathematical rules to be flagrantly disobeyed in everyday life is proportionality – the idea that, if it takes one man one week to dig a trench twelve feet long, it will take seven men just one day to dig the same trench. This of course does not hold in real life; seven men will take at least three times as long as one man would, depending on their union affiliations and demarcations, number of games of cards they play, etc.

Similarly, if it takes one bureaucrat twenty minutes to find your records on the file, you can be sure it will take five of them three hours. There is even a well-defined function $N_t(p)$, the number of people needed such that if they all look for p of your records they will lose them in t minutes. This function is of vital importance in deciding manning levels in the civil service.

At the innumerable points on the M1 where two lanes are shut off for vital purposes such as parking unused JCBs, stacking bollards, testing if two men can make a cup of tea twice as fast as one etc., the traffic funnels into the one remaining lane. Classical mechanics predicts that the speed of traffic flow should therefore increase threefold through that lane, which doesn't quite explain why a twenty-mile tailback forms immediately and everything reduces to a crawl.

There are occasions where proportionality does hold, contrary to mathematical prediction. For example, a four-piece jazz band and an eight-piece jazz band playing the same piece should take the same time as any schoolboy or girl could tell you, but in reality the eight-piece will take twice as long to let everyone have a solo.

Probability

Probability predicts many surprising things, none of which ever happens in real life, as you might expect. For example, the chance of getting a telephone call while you are in the shower is extremely small, but empirical evidence shows this to be a common occurrence. The chances of finding someone who knows the street you're trying to find in a strange town should be pretty high, but for some incredible reason the only people you ever meet are American tourists, imbeciles, and people who just moved there yesterday, events which should be extraordinarily remote.

Horse-racing gives many examples of the rules of probability being flouted. For a start, as you will point out whenever possible, the odds are quoted the wrong way round – 'two to one' really means one in three, or a third. Also, if you add up the odds on all the horses, the total should of course be one, because it is one hundred per cent certain that the race will be won by a horse. The fact that it never does shows how clever the bookies are at using mathematics creatively, siphoning off this discrepancy to buy BMWs and houses and holidays in Florida. Very few of them ever did the Number Theory option at university.

A very dubious application of probability is in life expectancy. When born you have a life expectancy of seventy-four or whatever. But, on reaching seventy-four as expected, you find your life expectancy is now eighty-six, and you can expect to live another twelve years. Similarly, on reaching eighty-six, you find you can expect to make it to ninety-four, and so on.

Weather forecasts in America give the chance of precipitation (rain) for the coming day – ten per cent, eighty per cent, and so on. Of course in England the chance of precipitation (rain) is always thirty per cent every day so the system is not used here, but should you get the chance, you can challenge people to say exactly what 'eighty per cent chance of precipitation (rain)' actually means. You can tell them, with a knowing smile, that it means in eighty per cent of places, there will very probably be rain (precipitation).

You must give the air of understanding the above two examples, but of deliberately presenting them in a misleading way; if you can do this you can get anyone else at a party worried that they can't work out exactly what it all means, which will almost certainly be the case – unless, of course they're an actuary, in which case they're not going to be invited to any good parties anyway, in all probability.

Statistics

The first problem with statistics is that they are often misinterpreted; if thirty per cent of all accidents are caused by drunken drivers, it means that seventy per cent are caused by sober ones, who are clearly therefore the greater danger. So you have to think about what the figures really mean, which nobody ever does, especially politicians. If a politician claims that we have had the biggest industrial growth of any of the major industrialised nations in the last six months, it probably means a) they have all grown so much they don't need to grow much faster and b) until six months ago we were stagnating, so our growth rate is impressive because we started out much smaller than anyone else.

Similarly 'the rate of inflation is coming down' still means prices are increasing, and tells you little except the rate is probably still too high and they're not going to tell you what it is.

Watch out for doctored graphs like those showing the 'dramatic' fall in the unemployment figures from 3,200,00 to 3,100,00, where the scale of people unemployed on the left of the graph starts at 3,000,000, thus making it look like the number has halved. If the graph started as it should, at zero, the effect would be no more than a dint out of a huge lump, but would not be nearly so impressive. This sort of rank cheat occurs all over the place and scores good points for the bluffer who points it out – if you ever see a graph with a scale not starting at zero, you can confidently expect that it's a fiddle.

Averages

You should know that the three types of commonly used averages are the **mean**, the **median** and the

mode. The mean is the average (like the cricket average, add up everything and divide by the number of things), the median is the middle term of the lot if they are arranged in order, and the mode is the most common one. So the 'average pay' in Britain could be quite different depending on which sort is used – the mean (which includes all the stockbrokers and actuaries and MPs) will give a high figure (so it is usually quoted by the Government), the mode will give a low figure (because most people earn a low salary, hence it is quoted by the opposition). The mean can often give misleading impressions, for example the mean number of children in Britain is 1.8 per family or whatever, the mode is 2. Always question a figure if it's quoted as an 'average' – "*Which* average? It makes all the difference, doesn't it?" – etc. Whichever one it is, make out that it should be one of the others.

Interest

Anything which gets bigger faster than you expect is called a **geometric progression**. Something which gets bigger faster than you'd expect, and goes on getting bigger faster and faster, is an **exponential increase**, though you never get those in real life. Not even the combined national debts of South America are increasing exponentially.

Be sure to say something impressive whenever people complain about credit card repayments – "Yes, they deliberately mislead you, because they quote you monthly rates, which are geometric means" – that sort of thing.

Population is another thing that tends to increase faster than you'd expect. By the year 2000, the world will no longer be able to be packed shoulder-to-shoulder on the Isle of Wight, and every other person will be either Chinese or Indian, a situation already true in many cities in England. Environmentally aware types will know that the ability of the earth to sustain life only increases **arithmetically** (i.e. about as quick as you'd expect) whereas the number of mouths to feed increases **geometrically**, "and I don't have to tell you what *that* means," you can say ominously.

Another equally ominous example of a geometric increase is the number of patients with some highly infectious disease. Start with one carrier, let him or her make five contacts, let those five contacts each have five contacts, and so on. Working out whether, combining the twin effects of population growth through lack of birth control and decrease through death by disease, the overall figure goes up or down, needs **differential equations**, and by this time you will have scared everyone sufficiently to stop them asking you what a differential equation is.

Geometry

By knowing the names of the various shapes one encounters you will give the impression of someone who knows and understands how things tick. Bluffers should know that the cables on suspension bridges, pulled down by the weight of the box sections, assume the form of **parabolas**, which, you will continue confidently, is the same shape as the reflectors in bicycle lamps and car headlights and electric heaters, as if the connection were obvious. In fact the connection is very tenuous – parabolas are used in lights because they reflect the light from the bulb into a straight beam, which is clearly nothing to do with suspension bridges at all.

However, any freely suspended ropes, cables or strings – washing-lines, for example, after the underwear has been stolen – take the shape of **catenaries**.

You will also mention in a throwaway fashion that the equation of a catenary is quite simple really, just "e to the x plus e to the minus x", as if you understand what you were saying, and as if anyone could tell the difference anyway.

Cooling towers at power stations are **hyperbolas** because, as you will point out, this shape can be constructed with steel girders; difficult as it is to believe, cooling towers are made entirely of straight girders, all of which link the top and bottom at a skewed angle. Whether you can visualise it or not, you must look as if you can, clearly and easily.

Snails' shells are **logarithmic spirals**, which have the odd property that they look the same from six inches as from a million miles away – and if the snails are in a really strong garlic sauce a million miles is probably the safer bet.

Remember that hyperbola and parabola, being Latin words, can take either -s or -e in the plural, and whichever the other person uses, you should correct them and say it's the other one.

The **circle** has many well-known properties such as occasionally being vicious, but is chiefly useful for its ability to serve as a wheel. The circumference of any circular shape, say a pie, divided by the diameter is always the same. According to the Bible this is 3. The Greeks knew it to be 3.1416, the value generally used today, and the number was called π. Since then things have gone downhill. The Italian Vieta calculated it to ten places of decimals in the 1500s, the German van Ceulen went to thirty-five and had them engraved on his tombstone; and recently, hours of valuable computer time have been wasted in calculating it to millions of places, when eight or so is quite accurate enough to be able to get to the moon.

You should know the mnemonic devised by Sir

James Jeans in which the number of letters in each word gives π:

How I want a drink, alcoholic of course, after the heavy lectures involving quantum mechanics (3.14159265358979).

A teetotal version exists beginning "May I have a large container of coffee . . . ", and obscene variations can often be found on the lavatory walls of mathematics faculties.

Relativity

Relativity is fertile ground for bluffers because the mathematics is so incredibly complex that everyone shies away from it, but the effects and consequences are so interesting that everyone likes to discuss it in superficially convincing 'man-in-the-street' terms without really knowing anything detailed about it at all, which is exactly what the bluffer aims to do.

First you point out that the mathematics of relativity is very, very complex, and quote the following story. When Einstein's theories were published, the famous English physicist Eddington was asked if it was true that he was only one of three people in the world who understood it, and his silence was first taken to be a sign of modesty. In fact Eddington was trying to think who the third person could possibly be.

Having established this you can claim smilingly to a 'rough appreciation' of some of the effects. Einstein's **Theory of Special Relativity** in 1905 concerned the effects for two observers moving relative to each other and showed that each one thinks the other's watch is slow, their rulers are too short, and they're putting on weight, but that they themselves are quite normal. This obviously flies in the face of reality where people who *don't* move relative to anything are usually the ones who put on weight. If your audience can keep up that far you can fox them completely by stressing that all these effects are relative.

Einstein's **Theory of General Relativity** in 1916 went further and showed that gravity distorts the space-time continuum, a phrase you should use constantly if you want to sound convincing, such that clocks tick slower near large gravitational sources, meaning that fat people's watches are liable to be wrong. (A particularly effective trick here is to make sure your own timepiece is slightly fast and challenge a weighty individual to compare times). Time moves fractionally, but with sophisticated instruments measurably, slower on the lower floors of buildings, for example, because they're nearer to the earth, and moves especially slowly in the ground floors of office blocks between three-thirty and five o'clock on Fridays.

If some bright spark tries to test you by hinting at the famous equation $E=mc^2$ you should smile in a superior way and remind them that that particular equation was not big news and was known pretty well before Einstein. It was, you note regrettably, the basis of atom bomb theory. The whole business of using mathematics to kill people is so depressing the conversation will go no further and you can retire with your total ignorance of what $E=mc^2$ actually represents unchallenged.

Topology

You preface any comment on topology by saying it is one of the new and interesting areas of mathematics, both these terms being extremely relative. Topology asks you to consider that everything is made of plasticene and rubber sheets and it sounds as if it was designed by perverts. Topologists are a downtrodden lot and are fed up with hearing the joke that to make a rubber ball topologically equivalent to a sheet it only takes a prick.

The first topology problem was about the possibility of crossing all the bridges to an island in Konigsberg in one journey without going over the same bridge twice, and from there it has progressed to the theory of colouring maps and fastening locks and tying knots, further evidence that it was designed for perverts as well.

A famous little topology problem is trying to join every one of three houses to each of three outhouses without the paths crossing; it is impossible.

You can quote maps as "good examples of topology" and that Greenland always looks so big and so icy, cold, barren and glacier-ridden because of the distortion encountered when you try and flatten a globe onto a map (but say "represent a sphere in two dimensions" – it sounds better).

A good topological theorem to mention any time is the theorem which, in essence, states that however you try to comb the hair on a hairy ball, you can never do it smoothly – the so-called 'hairy ball' theorem. You can make snide comments about the grooming of the party hosts' dog or cat in the meantime as you pick the hairs off your trouser leg.

The Golden Number

A number which crops up everywhere is $(\sqrt{5}+1)/2$, or $1.618\ldots$ This number is the solution to various problems in mathematics but its chief importance is that a rectangle with its sides in this ratio seems to be the most pleasing shape possible, and it can be found in architecture everywhere, except of course modern architecture. You can impress people enormously by measuring the height and width of any pleasing rectangular shape (say a piece of paper) and showing that when you divide one by the other you get 1.618. You can blow their minds completely by adding that according to one survey the ratio of a woman's height to the height of her navel above the ground is, surprise surprise, 1.618 . . .

Counting

Tenuous though the link with real mathematics is, you will probably end up having to do some bluffing on numbers sooner or later.

The system of counting on fingers is not as universal as you might think – in Japan it's the number of fingers you don't hold up which determines the number you are trying to express, and the signs for 1,2,3 etc. are the same as those for 9,8,7, which makes you wonder how on earth the Japanese are far and away the best mathematicians in the world.

At the other end of the scale there is the eternal confusion between the American system of counting with its characteristic New World hyperbole in which 1 000 000 000 is a billion, where in the UK it would only be a thousand million. This system carries on so that, for example, a US trillion is only a billion in the UK. All these figures are never used except in military research where money is no object anyway (as in the reputed quote of Caspar Weinberger of the US Defence Budget: 'A billion here, a billion there – it all adds up') and in Italy for buying houses, cars, stamps etc. Regrettably the US system seems to be supplanting the UK version so that politicians can claim to have spent nearly a billion on the Health Service when the previous lot only spent a miserable nine hundred and eighty million.

In the Orient people count in units of ten thousand and not thousands as in the West, hence they call a million 'one hundred ten-thousands'. In Japan, for example, they call a millionaire a ten-thousand-aire, a fountain pen a ten-thousand-year-brush, and toast each other with 'banzai', which means 'ten thousand years.'

In India it is even worse, and they count in units of one hundred thousand and ten million in a desperate bid to keep the population figures down.

When it comes to counting floors the US and Japan are also out of step with the eminently more sensible British system; they call the first floor the second floor, the ground (noughth) floor the first floor and the first floor basement the first floor basement, leaving an ugly jump from +1 to –1, which is very unmathematical, like not having a zero marked on a thermometer.

In France there are, with characteristic Gallic nonconformism, four hundred degrees in a circle. They call them centigrades and so get into all sorts of trouble when foreigners start quoting temperatures.

Calculating

The system we learn in the West for multiplication is by no means the best. Calculating prodigies who can multiply 6483976 by 55601243 in their head in ten seconds use a variety of shortcuts 'so simple kids can do them easily but adults can't', meaning that only a child would be naive enough to think that being able to multiply 6483976 by 55601243 in their head in twenty seconds was a really cool thing to be able to do.

The Greeks, with their cumbersome way of writing calculations down longhand, used to do their sums by moving little stone balls around in grooves in the sand (hence, from the Greek word for stone ball, calculus, comes our word for not only 'calculate' but also 'calculus', which many people regard as a load of that).

You can impress a lot of people by showing them an alternative way of multiplying which only uses addition and dividing by two "known to the ancients for centuries" (rubbish, naturally).

Suppose you are multiplying 29 by 13. Draw two columns on the restaurant tablecloth or dashboard or message pad and put 29 at the top of the left and 13 at the top of the right. Down the 29 column, keep halving and ignoring remainders ("the ancients didn't understand fractions"), so that you end up with a column reading 29, 14, 7, 3, 1. Then double the 13 the same number of times, so you get a column reading 13, 26, 52, 104, 208. Then say that the ancients believed even numbers in the left-hand column, together with their right-hand partners, were evil, or some such nonsense, and cross out the 14 and its partner 26. Add up the remaining 13, 52, 104, and 208 and you get 377, the answer, as if by magic.

Do not attempt to explain why this works (and it always does), but smile smugly and say "It's obvious once you see it". You can even go further and claim that children always think it's obvious but adults can't see it because they've been blinkered by education. Absolute rot of course – most kids would lose interest after five seconds and just start picking their noses – but excellent for getting people to worry about the decline in their faculties.

PUZZLES AND TEASERS

There is always someone at a party who takes pleasure in asking mindbending brainteasers. These are the sort of people who used to shout 'Your back wheel's moving' at cyclists when they were young. Fortunately there are only a few, and they are always asked in the same form – the answers are outlined below. You can try two approaches; either pretend you are actually working out the answer and get it in a mock flash of inspiration, or give the answer before they've finished asking the question, alternatively even before they've started. In practice the last is more impressive and gets rid of people faster.

The Lying Natives
You are asked to imagine the preposterous scenario of being in the jungle where there are two tribes, one which always tells the truth, the other which always lies. You come to a fork in the road and want to know which road leads to the town, but do not know which tribe the native sitting by the roadside belongs to. What question do you ask?

The usual answer – "If I asked you if this road led to the town, would you say 'yes'?" – is ridiculous as no self-respecting liar would get taken in by such a cheap tactic. The liar's aim is to deceive, and he or she won't be put off by logical tricks. Instead you could try something like "Did you know that there's free beer today in the town?" The truth teller will say no and run off down the road to town; the liar will say yes and run off down the road to town.

Of course a really professional liar would say yes and stay put, or run off down the wrong road deliberately, but you would have the consolation of making him or her worry that they were missing out on the free beer.

The Barber
The barber in a certain town shaves all the people who don't shave themselves. Who shaves the barber?

This is meant to be a clever little paradox with no solution but you can annoy the asker intensely by saying it's easy and the barber is a woman.

You can then ask the following (a version of Russell's **Paradox**, point this out too): in a library there are some books which list themselves in their bibliographies and some which don't. A librarian binds up a new book for the catalogue section which is a list of all books which don't list themselves. Should he or she include this book in its own list? If so, then it becomes a book which lists itself, so it shouldn't be in the list of books which don't, and vice versa. This should keep the most determined assailant at bay while you attack the wine.

The Mixed Red and White Wine
There are two glasses of wine, one white and one red. A teaspoonful of wine is taken from the red and mixed in with the white. Then a teaspoonful of this mixture is taken and mixed in with the red. Which is bigger, the amount of red in the white, or the amount of white in the red?

The answer is that they're both the same, because there's the same volume in each glass, so whatever quantity of red is in the white must be equal to the quantity of white in the red. However in practice it is impossible to do this because the white always runs out first at parties and the red always gets spilt on someone's white trousers.

The Chess Board
An Indian pundit beat a Maharajah at chess, and for his reward, demanded a grain of rice on the first square, two on the second, four on the third, eight on

the fourth, and so on. How much rice did the Maharajah give?

The answer is $2^{64}-1$, more rice even than the EEC could envisage surplusing. A similar problem asks you to say how thick a piece of paper folded sixty-four times is, and the answer is always "Higher than the moon".

The Socks
You have a wardrobe full of fifty black and fifty white socks which, to add a touch of realism, is in a pitch-black room. How many socks must you take to make sure of getting a pair the same colour?

The answer is three in theory, though everyone says fifty-one. In practice the answer is one hundred because most of them will have holes in anyway.

The Hotel Clerk
A hotel clerk is fixing the numbers on the hotel doors for all the rooms from one to one hundred. How many figure nines are required?

The answer is twenty, but in practice some 9s get put up as 6s and vice-versa so the real figure could be anything.

The Pond
A pond doubles its size every day. On the twelfth day it stops. On what day was it half-full?

The eleventh.

With global warming, the question can be revised so the pond halves its size every day.

GLOSSARY

There are many innocent words in English, the most useful of which are listed below, which have been appropriated by mathematicians and used for their own peculiar ends (this being an affliction quite common among closeted academics). Sprinkle your conversation with these words or double meaning and you will impress both the non-mathematicians (who will think you're using the word in its mathematical sense) and the mathematicians (who will think you're using the word in its everyday sense and making a subtle pun on the mathematical reference).

Algorithm – Not 'a logarithm' but any sneaky calculating trick – clearly, because of the al-, ('the' in Arabic) a word coined by Arabic mathematicians, i.e. al-gorithm (as in al-batross, al-chemy, al-cohol, al-gebra, and al-paca).

Argument – Name given to the angle a complex number makes with real numbers to disguise the fact that traditionally mathematicians have insulted each other whenever possible.

Calculators – Time-saving device for doing sums which in particular means one can find eleven twelves without chanting the entire twelve times table, and is hence considered a mark of decline by the older generation.

Chaos – Exciting new area of mathematics which deals in being able to say just when something unpredictable is going to happen.

Chess – Physical exercise for pure mathematicians.

Complex number – a) the hybrid offspring of a real number and an imaginary number b) any number too difficult to remember offhand.

Discrete space – Pretend world in which everything is exactly the same distance from everything else, thus ensuring everyone has equal privacy.

Differentials – Infinitesimally small increases in something which actually make a big difference, as in pay differentials.

Excluded third – The idea that everything is either true or false. The validity of this theorem is highly disputed in Whitehall.

Fluid mechanics – The study of the movement of fluids, especially liquids in metal cylinders which come in fours.

Group theory – An exceedingly beautiful branch of pure mathematics used for showing how many different ways blocks of wood can be painted.

Hyperbolic functions – Hyperbolic equivalents (shin, chos, than) of the circular functions (sin, cos, tan) which have a vastly exaggerated and over-rated importance.

Identity – Any member of a group which has no discernible effect on any of the others – zero in addition, for example, or one in multiplication – this characterises the typical mathematical identity.

Imaginary number – A pretend answer to an equation that otherwise wouldn't have any solutions, like the square root of minus one – so called because it is impossible to imagine what on earth it all means.

Integration – Something that mathematicians perfected hundred of years before the concept of a multicultural society.

Intuition – Claiming something you can't actually prove is obvious.

Irrational number – A number which cannot be expressed by any fraction, like the square root of two, and keeps appearing irrationally in problems where it is least expected.

Lemma – A condition affecting mathematics students whereby they prove things before starting on the main proof of a theorem; those who cannot remember which of two lemmas they are supposed to use are said to be in a dilemma.

Logarithms – Colloquially known as 'logs' in a desperate attempt to wrestle some humour out of this tedious calculating device.

Matrix – A set of figures arranged into rows and columns, like a league table – from the Latin word matrix meaning 'womb'.

Natural numbers – Numbers with no additives and nothing taken away. Also called whole numbers.

Operations research – The mathematical study of efficiency in technical processes, the usual conclusion of which is that the operations researchers will have to go.

Partial differentials – Differentials biased towards one of x, y, or z instead of treating all three equally – the sign for this is a six written the wrong way round.

Perfect number – A number which is just too good to be true, like 28.

Prime number – A number with no divisors. Boxes of chocolates always contain a prime number so that, whatever the number of people present, somebody has to have that one left over.

Pure mathematician – Anyone who prefers set theory to sex.

Quadratic – Something with x^2s, xs and numbers in it. If it also contains x^3 then it's cubic. If there's anything involving x^7 it's septic.

Rational number – The official name for a fraction, so called because, if you take all the fractions there are and share them out between an infinite number of people, you can ration them out exactly.

Real number – Any number, including those in the cracks between the fractions like root two and π. The real numbers are dense; unlike the rationals, they cannot be shared out completely between even an infinite number of people, and you'd have to be really dense to try it.

Repeating decimal – A group of numbers which recurs for ever when you try to write some fractions as decimals. So named because the only real example of this, the fact that one-seventh when written as a decimal is 0.142857 142857 142857 142 ... etc, is repeated ad nauseam in popular books on mathematics.

Ring – A ring is somewhere between a field and a group. You can talk blithely about embedding rings in fields and it means something quite complicated in mathematics.

Roots – Values of x which make the equation true. Like many discriminated-against and misunderstood minorities, mathematicians are always searching for their roots.

Set of all sets – Now frowned upon concept of early set theory which included in its members a third of a game of tennis, a hairdo, a tea service and a badger's hideout.

Sin, cos, tan, cot, sec, cosec – Formulae derived from

the sides of triangles but which crop up in completely unexpected places. Sins are extremely common but rarely do you encounter secs in mathematics.

Solid mechanics – Branch of mathematics concerned with the behaviour of solids under stress and deformation, especially metal cylinders with ring-pulls.

Solitons – Waveform modelling concept, short for solitary waves. A way of describing the motion of someone's hand as they say goodbye on the train platform.

Surds – Irrational numbers you tread in.

Topology – A branch of mathematics in which an apple and a banana are equivalent because everything is made of rubber.

Transcendental number – A number which is not the root of any equation, like π and e, and which can only be understood after several hours' meditation in the lotus position.

Undecidability – The theory which says it is impossible to construct a machine to decide if things are true or false on purely logical grounds, and which therefore renders the existence of Mr Spock highly questionable.

THE AUTHOR

Robert Ainsley was born in 1961 in Hull, a city inexplicably twinned not with some industrial town on the Ruhr, but with Freetown, Sierra Leone.

His final maths exams at the Queen's College, Oxford, amazed his tutors – not because they were any good but because it was the first time most of them had heard of him. He trained as a teacher and made a significant contribution to mathematics education by leaving it immediately, then lived for a while in Japan and became a millionaire, but only in yen.

Now resident in Bath, he writes for the music magazine *Classic CD,* proving that ability in music and maths are often absent in equal proportions.

THE BLUFFER'S GUIDES

Available at £1.95 and (new editions) £1.99 each

Accountancy	Management
Advertising	Marketing
Antiques	Maths
Archaeology	Modern Art
Ballet	Motoring
Bird Watching	Music
Bluffing	Occult
British Class	Opera
The Classics	Paris
Computers	Philosophy
Consultancy	Photography
Cricket	Poetry
EEC	Public Speaking
Espionage	Publishing
Feminism	Racing
Finance	Seduction
Fortune Telling	Sex
Golf	Teaching
Green	Television
Hi-Fi	Theatre
Hollywood	Top Secretaries
Japan	University
Jazz	Weather Forecasting
Journalism	Wine
Literature	World Affairs

All these books are available at your local bookshop or newsagent, or can be ordered direct from the publisher. Just tick the titles you require and fill in the form below. Prices and availability subject to change without notice.

Ravette Books Limited, 3 Glenside Estate, Star Road, Partridge Green, Horsham, West Sussex RH13 8RA.

Please send a cheque or postal order, and allow the following for postage and packing: UK 27p for one book and 15p for each additional book ordered.

Name ....

Address..

....

....